A NOTE TO PARENTS

Reading Aloud with Your Child

Research shows that reading books aloud is the single most valuable support parents can provide in helping children learn to read.

- Be a ham! The more enthusiasm you display, the more your child will enjoy the book.
- Run your finger underneath the words as you read to signal that the print carries the story.
- Leave time for examining the illustrations more closely; encourage your child to find things in the pictures.
- Invite your youngster to join in whenever there's a repeated phrase in the text.
- Link up events in the book with similar events in your child's life.
- If your child asks a question, stop and answer it. The book can be a means to learning more about your child's thoughts.

Listening to Your Child Read Aloud

The support of your attention and praise is absolutely crucial to your child's continuing efforts to learn to read.

- If your child is learning to read and asks for a word, give it immediately so that the meaning of the story is not interrupted. DO NOT ask your child to sound out the word.
- On the other hand, if your child initiates the act of sounding out, don't intervene.
- If your child is reading along and makes what is called a miscue, listen for the sense of the miscue. If the word "road" is substituted for the word "street," for instance, no meaning is lost. Don't stop the reading for a correction.
- If the miscue makes no sense (for example, "horse" for "house"), ask your child to reread the sentence because you're not sure you understand what's just been read.
- Above all else, enjoy your child's growing command of print and make sure you give lots of praise. *You are your child's first teacher — and the most important one. Praise from you is critical for further risk-taking and learning.*

— Priscilla Lynch
Ph.D., New York University
Educational Consultant

For Gilda with love,
L'Chaim!
—J. Marzollo

To my friends,
Matthew and Harrison
—J. Moffatt

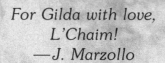

Text copyright © 1997 by Jean Marzollo.
Illustrations copyright © 1997 by Judith Moffatt.
All rights reserved. Published by Scholastic Inc.
HELLO READER!, CARTWHEEL BOOKS, and the CARTWHEEL BOOKS logo
are registered trademarks of Scholastic Inc.

Library of Congress Cataloging-in-Publication Data

Marzollo, Jean.
    I'm a caterpillar / by Jean Marzollo ; illustrated by Judith Moffatt.
      p.   cm. — (Hello reader! Level 1)
    Summary: Provides a simple explanation of what happens as a caterpil-
lar changes into a butterfly — from the caterpillar's point of view.
    ISBN 0-590-84779-1
    1. Caterpillars — Juvenile literature. 2. Butterflies — Life cycles —
Juvenile literature. [1. Caterpillars. 2. Butterflies. 3. Metamorphosis.]
I. Moffatt, Judith, ill. II. Title. III. Series.
QL544.2.M26   1997
595.78 ' 043—dc20   96-26744
                                                 CIP
                                                 AC
24 23 22 21 20 19 18 17 16   2/0

Printed in the U.S.A.   24

First Scholastic printing, March 1997

I'm a Caterpillar

by Jean Marzollo
Illustrated by Judith Moffatt

Hello Science Reader ! — Level 1

SCHOLASTIC INC.

Cartwheel
·B·O·O·K·S·®

New York   Toronto   London   Auckland   Sydney

I'm a caterpillar.
Munch.
Crunch.

I'm getting bigger!
Munch.
Crunch.

Munch. Crunch.
Munch. Crunch.

That's it.
No more food.
I'm done.

It's time to hang from a stem.

I wait,
and wait,
and wait.

I shiver.
I twist.
I split my skin!

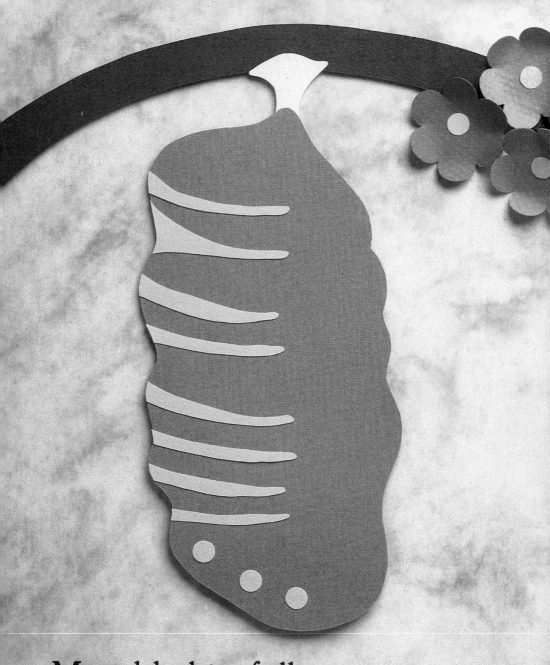

My old skin falls away.
I am soft inside.
I am a pupa (PEW-pah).

I grow a shell
to protect the pupa.
I am now a chrysalis
(KRIS-ah-lis).

I keep changing.
Soon I'll come out.
What will I be?

A butterfly!
Push.
Crack.
Wow!
I'm free!

My wings are all wet.

My wings dry off.
They unfold.

Flap. Flap.
Hey!
I can fly!
Ta-da!

I visit flowers.
I drink nectar.
Yum!

My mouth is like
a straw.
Sip.
Sip.
Sip.

I have a mate.
We visit many flowers.

We're not afraid of birds.
They know that
we taste awful.

Soon I will lay my eggs.

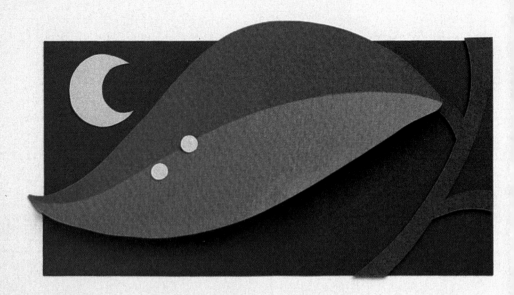

The eggs have thin shells.

Baby caterpillars crawl out.

Hi! I'm a caterpillar.

Munch. Crunch.

caterpillar

What will happen
to me next?
Do you know?

chrysalis

butterfly

eggs